KIERKEGAARD
THE MELANCHOLY DANE

KIERKEGAARD

THE MELANCHOLY DANE

By

H. V. MARTIN
M.A., B.D., Ph.D.

PHILOSOPHICAL LIBRARY
NEW YORK

INTRODUCTION

MANY people have heard of the name of Sören Kierkegaard but they do not profess to know very much about him. We come across references to him in modern religious books. We even hear him quoted on the wireless in religious addresses. But who exactly was he? What did he stand for? What was his significance? Has he any message for the world of today? For the man who is eager to be abreast of modern thought, and who is searching for more light amidst the confusion of the age, an understanding of the main points of Kierkegaard's work is essential.

Kierkegaard's own writings are now available in English translations; but they are so voluminous, and at the first reading so difficult, that not everyone will have the time and patience to persevere right through to the end. In the following pages, an attempt is made to tell the story of Kierkegaard and to present his main thoughts within a brief compass and in a connected manner. Any such attempt is fraught with many dangers, not the least of which is the fact that Kierkegaard's viewpoint is not presented in the form of a system which we can take over ready-made. There are no final results given for our verdict. Kierkegaard demands that each one of us wrestle for himself with the vital problems of life which he wrestled with, and which can be solved only in the individual life by actual living. The hope of the present writer is that the discerning reader will be so stimulated, and that the challenge of the Christian life will come home with a new force through Kierkegaard's exposition of what it means to be a Christian.

Kierkegaard is rapidly becoming one of the outstanding figures in the world of modern thought. Whether we can agree in any measure with his outlook or not, we shall have to admit that he cannot and should not be ignored. As Höffding remarks: 'Every important individuality is a point of view for the human race from which men catch sight of possibilities and aspects of existence which would otherwise have escaped them.' If we can stand where Kierkegaard stood, we may catch glimpses of a far-stretching vista which will bring strength to endure and encouragement to go on, as we labour from day to day in the dark vales of human tragedy.

NOTE.—The sub-title of this book is derived from the Preface of Dr. P. T. Forsyth's *The Work of Christ*, where he refers to Kierkegaard as 'the melancholy Dane in whom Hamlet was mastered by Christ'.

H. V. M.

CORES END,
  BOURNE END,
    BUCKS.

KIERKEGAARD'S BOOKS IN ENGLISH TRANSLATIONS

WITH ABBREVIATIONS USED

LIST OF BOOKS IN ENGLISH ON KIERKEGAARD

CHAPTER ONE

A GENIUS IN A PROVINCIAL TOWN

Therefore, some day, not only my writings, but my whole
life . . . will be studied and studied.—THE JOURNALS, 715

THE LIFE-STORY of Sören Kierkegaard provides
material of intense interest both for the religious
psychologist and for the Christian theologian. From the
human point of view his life appears as a sad tragedy.
What human happiness was, he never knew. His days
were spent in laborious writing, in inward struggles, and
in lonely misunderstanding. Yet never was a life more
victorious in the end or more justified by the verdict of
posterity.

Sören Kierkegaard was born on 5th May 1813, in
Copenhagen, the capital of Denmark, the seventh and
youngest child of Michael Kierkegaard, a retired mer-
chant in affluent circumstances. At the time of Sören's
birth, his father was fifty-six years old; and as Israel
loved Joseph more than all his children because he was
the son of his old age, so between Sören and his father
there was a bond of attachment which became one of the
great factors in the mental and spiritual development of
the son.

Michael Kierkegaard was a man of deep religious
earnestness and piety who brought up his children under
a strict and rigorous discipline. Underneath his sternness
and melancholy, there lay hidden a tragic fear. It
appears that as a boy, forced by his poverty to herd the
flocks on the heaths of Jutland, he had one day in the
misery of his hunger and want, stood on a hill and cursed
God. Shortly afterwards he had been adopted by a
relative, taken to Copenhagen, and initiated into business.

In this he prospered so well that he was able to retire in middle life with a fair fortune. Instead of returning his curse upon him, God had smiled upon him in material things beyond all his desires. In this, Michael Kierkegaard saw the sure sign of God's wrath, fearing that he had sinned against the Holy Ghost. With deep humility and repentance, he sought after forgiveness with tears throughout his life, consumed with inward fear and anguish of soul. Not only this; but after his first wife had died, in a moment of temptation, he had entered into illegitimate connexion with his maidservant, finally having to marry her to save her name. She was Sören's mother.

When he was seventeen years of age, young Sören entered the University at Copenhagen to study theology with a view to entering the ministry of the Church. This was at his father's express wish. But the strict religious upbringing of his home led to a reaction, and for the first five years Sören does not seem to have studied with any great earnestness, at least, not in the more serious subjects of his course. Never short of money, he lived a free and careless student-life with his friends.

In 1835, at the age of twenty-two, the young Kierkegaard began to have more serious thoughts of life. This did not last very long, for soon he began to throw himself wildly into all manner of dissipation until his parents and friends almost despaired of him. From his *Journals*, a kind of diary and scrap-book which he kept all his life, we discover that this wild outbreak was associated with the disclosure of the secret of his father's life. The shock of knowing the weakness and guilt of the one to whom he had always looked up in veneration and respect, so unnerved him that there were times when he even contemplated suicide. In a way that was typical of his nature, he hid his despair under a mask of extreme frivolity and gaiety, spending his nights at student parties where he was often the central figure with his sparkling wit and caustic humour. His bills mounted up; and about this time, his father had to pay off Sören's debts to the extent of about £600.

Gradually, however, things quietened down, and Sören became reconciled again to his father and went back to live at home. In fact, now that the secret was out, an even deeper bond sprang up between father and son, each conscious of an incurable melancholy of life. In 1838, when Sören was about twenty-five years of age, he passed through his first spiritual crisis, helped by the sympathetic understanding of his father, now an old man of eighty-one. An entry in the *Journals* for that year reads: 'How I thank you, Father in heaven, that you have preserved my earthly father here upon earth for a time such as this when I so greatly need him, a father who, as I hope, will with your help have greater joy in being my father the second time than he had the first time in being so.'[1]

Kierkegaard always maintained in his later life that he had never, even in his wildest days, rejected Christianity as untrue. He had been confirmed in the Danish State Church at the age of fifteen by Mynster, the favourite priest of his father. But it was ten years later before he definitely entered into a personal experience of Divine grace, and resolved to devote his life to the service of the Gospel. In the same month of July 1838 he registers his decision: 'I mean to labour to achieve a far more inward relation to Christianity; hitherto I have fought for its truth while in a sense standing outside it.'[2] It would seem that in the Divine Providence, his father had been preserved for this critical event; for, a month later, in August 1838, he died.

This was a terribly harrowing event for Sören; but again, he hid his grief from everyone. He never forgot his father, and the memory of the old man remained with the son as a constraining and inspiring influence. He admits that he owed everything to his father, despite the strained and abnormal atmosphere of the home, and his own upbringing. 'An old man, himself prodigiously melancholy, had a son in his old age upon whom the whole of that melancholy descended in inheritance.'[3] Sören never had any normal childhood of fun and games and playmates. As a young man he became introspective and imaginative, sensitive and brooding, and shrank from intimate friendships. But his father's death had at least one immediate result. It drove Sören to his studies, determined to fulfil his father's wishes and to prepare himself for the ministry of the Church.

About this time the second great formative influence of his life began to play its part. This was his engagement of marriage to Regine Olsen in 1840. She was the young daughter of a State Councillor, and at that time about seventeen years of age. They were both deeply in love with each other, and, for a short time, they were extremely happy. But Kierkegaard's melancholy broodiness, his natural secretiveness, and his polemical temperament, all unfitted him for a normal married life. When he first became engaged he had hoped that the loving companionship of this young girl would have healed his melancholy. Now he came to realize that this was impossible. His melancholy was rooted in a strong sense of religious guilt, which the strictness of his upbringing had enhanced. To him marriage meant frankness and openness, and the revealing to Regine both the family tragedy of his father, and his own sense of guilt before God. For the sake of her ultimate happiness he could not bring himself to this point, and so he decided that the engagement must be broken.

At first Regine would not agree. Thereupon Sören,

[3] J.600.

though still deeply in love with her, began deliberately to act indifferently toward her, so as to alienate her affections from him. He felt that it was God who was prohibiting the marriage; and this conviction alone prevented him from yielding to Regine's pleadings. In October 1841 the final break came, and Sören Kierkegaard, with the reproaches of his friends sounding in his ears, left Copenhagen for Berlin. This led to the second great religious crisis of his life. 'I had either to cast myself into perdition and sensuality, or to choose the religious absolutely as the only thing.'[4] Fortunately for posterity, he chose the latter; and in so choosing, he came to know that he had been called of God through the path of suffering to a decisive task.

In the period which followed, the nature of that task became clearer. He had already published his dissertation for his Master's degree in 1841, on *The Concept of Irony*. He now began to feel an irresistible urge to write; and from 1843 to 1846, some of his most important works were published. They were not published in his own name but under various pseudonyms. His aim was to present views of life concretely through the delineation of individual characters; and his poetic and dramatic gifts found their fullest scope in these brilliant psychological experiments. In addition to *Either/Or* (1843) there appeared in rapid succession *Repetition* (1843), *Fear and Trembling* (1843), a number of *Edifying Discourses*, (1843–5), *Philosophical Fragments* (1844), *The Concept of Dread* (1844), *Stages on Life's Way* (1845), and *The Concluding Unscientific Postscript* (1846). He soon became known throughout Denmark as a brilliant author; and though his more philosophical works were not widely read, his aesthetical works were greatly appreciated in the literary circles of the capital. Upon the death of his father, Sören had inherited considerable wealth. He

[4] *PV*.18.

B

could easily have obtained an appointment in the Church as a priest, but for the time being he preferred to devote himself to writing.

At the end of 1845, there arose another series of events which was destined to have great influence upon Kierkegaard's outlook. This was his conflict with the *Corsair*, a satirical and rather libellous periodical published in Copenhagen. Its manager was a young Jew named Goldschmidt, whose literary gifts Kierkegaard appreciated and wanted to see used in a better cause. Goldschmidt on his part liked Kierkegaard and had written in the *Corsair* with high praise of some of Kierkegaard's works. But the paper on the whole was a blot on the name of Copenhagen, and defamed and ridiculed the better-known people of the capital for the amusement of the vulgar. In December 1845 P. L. Möller, a former drinking companion of Kierkegaard in his more profligate days, wrote an article in a literary annual, criticizing rather superciliously one of Kierkegaard's books. Kierkegaard retaliated by a public letter in another paper expressing his contempt for Möller and his way of life, and hinting that Möller was at that time virtually editor of the *Corsair*. He also asked deliberately why he himself, alone amongst prominent Danish authors, had not yet been abused in that paper.

The revelation of Möller's secret connexion with the *Corsair* destroyed the hopes that he had of obtaining an official post in the University. So in revenge, Möller commenced a campaign of ridicule and slander against Kierkegaard in the pages of the *Corsair*. Articles were accompanied by caricatures, and this went on for many months. Kierkegaard was very sensitive to such ridicule, but he had hoped that his friends would rally round him in rooting out this libellous paper. They, however, were frightened of being lampooned themselves, and would scarcely be seen in public with him. In fact, the campaign

CHAPTER TWO

THE MORNING STAR OF A NEW REFORMATION

My merit in literature is that I have set forth the decisive qualifications of the whole compass of existence with such dialectical clarity and so originally as has not, so far as I know, been done in any other literature.

—THE JOURNALS, 601

DURING his own lifetime Kierkegaard's chief claim to fame lay in his more aesthetical writings. It is true that his religious discourses were appreciated by the more devout; but his larger philosophical and theological books received little recognition at all. He became notorious through the attack upon him in the *Corsair*, and Kierkegaard's own attack upon the Church in his last year of life made his name known throughout Scandinavia. During the last ten years of his life he was looked upon by the public as an eccentric religious recluse and unlikely to be remembered very long after his death.

An interesting contemporary account of Kierkegaard by a young Scot, Andrew Hamilton, is to be found in a book of travels: *Sixteen Months in the Danish Isles*, written in 1852. 'There is a man whom it is impossible to omit in any account of Denmark, but whose place it might be more difficult to fix; I mean Sören Kierkegaard. But as his works have, at all events for the most part, a religious tendency, he may find a place among the theologians. He is a philosophical Christian writer, evermore dwelling, one might almost say harping, on the theme of the human heart. There is no Danish writer more in earnest than he, yet there is no one in whose way stand more things to prevent his becoming popular. He writes at times with an unearthly beauty, but too often with an exaggerated display of logic that disgusts the public. . . . I have received the highest delight from some of his books. But no one of them could I read with pleasure all through. His *Works of Love* has, I suppose, been the most popular, or perhaps, his *Either/Or*, a very singular book. A little thing published during my stay, gave me much pleasure, *Sickness unto Death*. Kierkegaard's habits of life are singular enough to lend a (perhaps false) interest to his proceedings. He goes into no company, and sees nobody in his own house, which answers all the end of an invisible dwelling; I could never learn that anyone had been inside of it. Yet his one great study is human nature; no one knows more people than he. The fact is that he walks about town all day, and generally in some person's company; only in the evening does he write and read. When walking, he is very communicative, and at the same time manages to draw everything out of his companion that is likely to be profitable to himself. I do not know him. I saw him almost daily in the streets, and when he was alone, I often felt much inclined to accost him, but never put it into execution. I was told his talk was very fine. Could I have enjoyed it without the feeling that I was myself being mercilessly pumped and sifted, I should have liked very much.'

Of the excellence of Kierkegaard's literary style and language we have weighty testimony from his fellow-countrymen. Georg Brandes writes of Kierkegaard: 'Never before had Danish prose produced such wonderful works.' The Danish philosopher Höffding gives him equally high praise: 'Remarkably gifted as a poet and thinker . . . he clothed the possibilities of thought with an intuitive power and a richness of feeling unequalled in Danish literature.' Despite the beauty of his style, Kierkegaard's books are for the most part deep and difficult. His convictions were reached through the inward struggle of his own soul with God, and in the light of intense reflection upon human problems of life and thought. He was tried in daily life as few men of his sensitiveness have been tried; and out of it all, he brought forth a literature which not only appeals as 'deep unto deep', but which in its wider aspects has been instrumental in the birth of a new Reformation in Christian theology.

To the superficial reader, Kierkegaard's works will not generally appeal. He will seem to such, in the words of one critic, 'a poor, distracted, tormented soul'. Unless and until the reader feels kinship with Kierkegaard in the tragic problems of human life in relation to reality and to God, he may conclude as another critic has done, that 'his pathological state often reached the verge of insanity'. But to the man who is wrestling with the meaning of his existence and his destiny in the light of philosophy and religion, Kierkegaard will come with the Divine message of a fellow-pilgrim who has himself trodden the hard path of inward suffering, inseparable from a life deeply lived. As Dr. Bain writes: 'We feel that we are in contact with one to whom God and the soul and sin were intense realities. . . . Here was a soul aflame with the passion for God.'[1]

Many readers will at first find Kierkegaard's terminology difficult and confusing. But every great original thinker in the struggle to express his vital ideas as they come to birth in his soul, has to use new words, or to put new meaning into old terms. Speaking of Kierkegaard, Dr. H. R. Mackintosh writes: 'It is one mark of his power that, like Tertullian, he minted a new coinage.'[2] In fact, Kierkegaard's terminology is like a set of new instruments which are alone adequate to the new task. Dr. John A. Mackay brings out this point. 'Kierkegaard may be regarded as the representative thinker of our time, the man who faced our problems, and suffered vicariously

[1] B.116.   [2] MT.220.

for us in an abyss of misery, more than a hundred years
ago. . . . Like Dostoevsky, Kierkegaard sounded fathom-
less depths of anguish, and like the great Russian, he
forged in pain instruments which our generation finds
more adequate than any other to interpret its experience,
and orient its way in the present crisis of civilization.'[3]

Despite the little appreciation he received in his lifetime, Kierkegaard himself had a strong conviction of the
lasting value and importance of his work. Some of his
entries in the *Journals* will seem to English people very
strange by reason of their apparent pride and high self-
estimation. But Kierkegaard in this respect was too naïve
to be rightly accused of pride. With him it was the intense
realization of a Divine call to a special task, and the
Divine grace in equipping him for it. 'There is something
about me which points to greatness.'[4] Again: 'Where
intellectual gifts, knowledge, cast of mind are concerned,
there can be no doubt that I am properly endowed.'[5]

Here is no proud boasting, but a humble admission of
Divine favour. Kierkegaard was always a realist; and as
Andrew Hamilton pointed out, his great study was
human nature, and not least the study of his own heart.
'There has hardly been a poet before me with an equally
profound knowledge of life, and in particular of religion.'[6]
We should not judge Kierkegaard until at least we have
studied his conception of Divine Governance so remarkably expounded in his book, *The Point of View*. It was this
sense of Divine Governance which ruled Kierkegaard's
inner life.

That he was writing largely for posterity, and did not
expect to be appreciated in his own generation, is made
clear in many entries in the *Journals*. 'Oh, once I am
dead, *Fear and Trembling* alone will be enough to immor-
talize my name.'[7] He regretted in one sense that he was

a Dane and had to write in the Danish language; because this meant that it would take time for his ideas to spread into the wider world of European culture. He speaks of himself as 'a genius in a provincial town'.[8] He complains that if he had been born in any other country than Denmark, he would have been acclaimed as a genius of the first rank; whereas in Copenhagen he had become 'a sort of village idiot'.[9] But he is confident that time will do him justice, and that posterity would appreciate his work. So long as he was alive, he was a prophet, without honour in his own country. Only his death would place his work in the right perspective. 'My life will cry out after my death.'[10]

In the age during which Kierkegaard lived, the freshness of the influence of the Protestant Reformation had worn off. During the eighteenth century in Europe a cold Deism and Rationalism had overpowered the warmth of living religion in many countries. But the beginning of the nineteenth century had brought an age of great philosophical activity which was having great effect not only in the political life of Europe, but also in the reinterpretation and understanding of the Christian religion. It was in fact a second Renaissance. Only a few years before Kierkegaard was born, Immanuel Kant had passed away. Contemporary with Kierkegaard were the great figures of Hegel, Schleiermacher, Schopenhauer, and Feuerbach. When Kierkegaard died, Albrecht Ritschl was thirty-three years old.

Kierkegaard was closely in touch with the thought of his age. In the list of authors quoted by Kierkegaard in his *Journals*, we find, in addition to those mentioned above, the names of Fichte, Pascal, Fénelon, Abelard, Anselm, Augustine, Descartes, Goethe, Heine, Hoffman, Holberg, Victor Hugo, Lichtenburg, Montaigne, Rousseau, Spinoza, Tauler, Thomas à Kempis, Trendelenburg, and

Vinet. He was always a prolific reader of ancient and modern writers. In estimating the influence of other thinkers upon the development of Kierkegaard's own thought, whether in a positive or negative way, the names of Luther, Kant, Hegel, and Schleiermacher come immediately to mind. We will not deal with them here, since references will be made in considering the main ideas of Kierkegaard. It is sufficient to point out that philosophically and theologically, Kierkegaard was well equipped to treat with them on equal terms. Even with Hegel, whose massive system is generally considered involved and deep, Kierkegaard remarks, with a kind of serious humour, that the only passages where he could not understand him well, were those in which Hegel could not understand himself.[11] There are five other thinkers, however, who in their influence upon Kierkegaard demand a brief mention.

Kierkegaard was a proficient scholar in the classics of Ancient Greece and Rome. Amongst the great thinkers of the ancient world, there is no one to whom Kierkegaard is more indebted than to Socrates, the 'simple wise man' of Athens. Kierkegaard himself makes constant references to him in terms of the highest admiration. The principle that the ideal is to be found in the real, and not vice versa, Kierkegaard claims to have developed from Socrates; and thus arises his basic category of 'the existential' which he used so effectively against the abstract idealism of Hegel. From the 'maieutic' method of Socrates, though with significant changes due to the difference between the immanentism of Hellenism and the transcendentism of Christianity, Kierkegaard developed his concept of 'indirect communication' in connexion with the revelation of eternal truth. The stress upon the category of 'the individual' is another point of close contact. Just as Socrates used it to disintegrate Paganism, so Kierkegaard

[11] PV.39.

felt himself called to use it to 'reintroduce Christianity into Christendom'. Much of Kierkegaard's rooted aversion to Apologetics also comes from Socrates; for both of them stood for the position that eternal truth is not a communication of knowledge in an intellectual sense, but a communication of existence which is to be appropriated only by venturing out upon it in one's individual existence. Socrates was indeed a pagan. But Kierkegaard was convinced of his eternal salvation. 'It is true he was not a Christian, and yet I am thoroughly convinced that he has become one.'[12] Finally, the fact that Socrates, in spite of serving the cause of truth so wholeheartedly, was despised and condemned by his own generation, and only honoured after his death, served to energize Kierkegaard for his struggle with his own generation, and to comfort himself with the same hope.

Another thinker whose influence on Kierkegaard was considerable, but whose name is not widely known in English circles, was Georg Hamann, who died in 1788. He was known as 'The Magus of the North', since he lived at Königsberg at the same time as Kant. In temperament and outlook, Hamann differed widely from the great ethical philosopher. He had a strong feeling for the inner mystery of life, and for the contradictions encountered in existence when the finite understanding seeks to penetrate beneath appearances. He stressed the cleavage between reason and faith: 'Lies and novels must be plausible, also hypotheses and fables; but not the truths and fundamental propositions of our faith.' Real life, Hamann argued, is a coincidence of opposites, and must therefore be lived in continual tension. Here we find a link with Kierkegaard's stress upon the tension between faith and reason in relation to Christian revelation, and upon the truth that the Divine can only be truly expressed to the human in the form of Paradox. Kierkegaard also admired in Hamann

[12] PV.41.

the combination of deep seriousness and sparkling wit, an ideal which he kept before him in his own work. Finally, the lesson which he had learned from the life of Socrates, was confirmed by Hamann's book, *Living for Posterity*, which set forth the theme that to be misunderstood by one's contemporaries is a mark of greatness.

Another author whose work influenced Kierkegaard was Lessing (1729–81) who stressed the importance of the subjective inward striving after truth with his thesis: *The Chase is Better than the Prey*. From this Kierkegaard developed his own point that 'Truth is Subjectivity', a way of approach rather than a result to be taken over. In the *Postcript*, Kierkegaard deals at length with Lessing's dictum that contingent historical truths can never constitute a basis for the eternal truths of reason, and that the transition is always in the nature of a leap. Here Kierkegaard found seed-thoughts for his doctrine of the qualitative difference between time and eternity, for his concept of the eternal contemporaneousness of Christ, and for his definition of Christian faith as a leap of decision.

On the more personal side, Kierkegaard received great spiritual help in his first religious crisis of 1838 not only from his father, but also from his favourite professor at the Copenhagen University, Paul Martin Möller. It was he who constantly warned the young Kierkegaard against becoming too polemical.[13] Möller himself had been tried religiously by many doubts and difficulties, but he had won through at last to the serenity of Christian faith. He was therefore well qualified to help his young friend in his similar struggle from despair to faith. When Möller died in 1838, Kierkegaard promised himself never to forget him; and six years later, he dedicated *The Concept of Dread* to his memory, speaking of him as 'the mighty trumpet of my awakening'.

Toward the end of his life, Kierkegaard began to read

[13] J.1333/4.

with interest the works of Arthur Schopenhauer. Superficially, their outlook on many points was similar, as Kierkegaard himself recognizes. 'Arthur Schopenhauer is unquestionably an important writer, he has interested me very much, and I am astonished to find an author who, in spite of complete disagreement, touches me at so many points.'[14] Both stressed the misery of human existence, but for different reasons. Whereas Schopenhauer had nothing to offer but the negative solution of the renunciation of the will-to-live, Kierkegaard could point to the positive leap of Christian faith which raises man into the resurrection of a new life. Kierkegaard also approved of Schopenhauer's insight that self-denial is the essence of New Testament Christianity as compared with the easy-going, world-affirming attitude of modern Protestantism. It has also been suggested that Kierkegaard's tendency in his later years to disparage woman and marriage, is due to Schopenhauer's influence. This, however, is extremely doubtful. Long before coming across the works of Schopenhauer, Kierkegaard was convinced that in the light of Christianity, celibacy is a higher state than marriage, and that from the point of view of spiritual development, woman in marriage tends to bind a man to finite things. At the most, therefore, Schopenhauer's influence is limited to the hardening expression of Kierkegaard's already established ideas on this point.

These and many other influences had their part to play in the development of Kierkegaard's particular understanding of Christianity. But his originality is seen in the way in which, by his own creative insight, he rose above his necessary limitations as a child of his own day. His individual passion of soul and mind fused the vague and indeterminate seed-thoughts of others into a new whole, as he sought to bring out in his writings the true meaning of Christianity and of the Christian life. He was in his

[14] J.1319.

essential outlook not a man of his day. He lived before his time; and as Wyclif has been hailed as the Morning Star of the Protestant Reformation, so we may hail Kierkegaard as the Morning Star of a New Reformation in Christian Theology, the beginnings of which are now becoming apparent in this our own generation.

unrestricted possibilities by the "Thou".[7] The ethical life is the life of relationship in mutual obligation and responsibility; and it is in the community of common need that the ethical man finds the sphere and the inspiration for the development of personal character. 'Adversity draws men together and produces beauty and harmony in life's relationships, just as the cold of winter produces ice-flowers on the window-pane which vanish with the warmth.'[8]

THE RELIGIOUS STAGE

After presenting its dilemma of the aesthetical or the ethical, *Either/Or* closes with a sermon supposedly written by a country priest. It is entitled: 'Ultimatum', and its theme is 'the blessedness of the thought that before God, we are always in the wrong'. This suggests at once the question whether the ethical ideal painted so persuasively by the Judge is actually attainable by man. From a higher standpoint, i.e. before God, is not the ethical man equally in the wrong with the aesthetical man?

In one sense, the ethical ideal is at the same time the religious ideal, for religion does not supersede ethics but expresses the obligation of the universal in a different form. 'The ethical is the universal, and as such it is also the divine. It is therefore true to say that all duty is fundamentally duty toward God.'[9] The ethical man, assenting to the absolute claim of the moral law of his being, is faced with the task of expressing this absolute in his relative existence. The guiding principle, according to Kierkegaard, must be this: 'Relate thyself absolutely to absolute ends, and relatively to relative ends.'[10]

The ethical law, whether considered as the universal or as the divine, is absolute and unconditional. But man himself is a synthesis of time and eternity, of the particular and the universal, and of the relative and the absolute.

---

[7] *Man in Revolt* (E.T.), p. 265.   [8] *J*.37.   [9] *FT*.97.   [10] *CUP*.364.

He is neither an animal nor a disembodied spirit. Thus arises the dilemma of ethics. By his very nature man seems forced either to relate himself relatively to the absolute, or absolutely to the relative. To relate himself absolutely to the absolute, he would be forced out of the world of men and driven as an ascetic to the mountain top; but in so doing, he denies the claim of the relative. If, on the other hand, he lives in the world of men and holds to his relative duty to man, he cannot fulfil his absolute obligation to God and to the universal. 'I ought, therefore I can' may be a postulate of the moral sense of man; but in actual human existence man finds that he cannot fulfil the absolute in the relative. The ethical ideal is beyond him. Therefore, if he is sincere, he falls into ethical despair, and this points him beyond the ethical stage to a special religious relationship in Divine grace.

The religiousness to which the ethical dilemma points is not the general religiousness natural to mankind as a whole. That kind of religiousness goes hand in hand with ethics as the universal of duty. The special religious relationship of which Kierkegaard speaks is on the contrary one which involves the teleological suspension of the universal ethical, at least, as a possibility. He brings this out in an examination of the typical case of Abraham and Isaac, and of the nature of Abraham's faith. This we shall consider more fully later on. It is sufficient here to stress that this difference between general ethico-religiousness and the paradoxical religiousness of Biblical Christianity is vital to the right understanding of Kierkegaard's thought.

Kierkegaard, unlike Barth, is not afraid to admit the possibility of natural religion and natural theology. To him it is based upon an immediate relationship to the Divine, as immanent in man and in creation. This natural religiousness arises in man through a sense of wonder at that which is beyond his grasp or comprehension. 'Wonder is the sense immediacy has of God and is the beginning of all deeper understanding.'[11] In this sense God is the inexplicable ALL of existence, and is apprehended only as the great UNKNOWN. Human reason cannot pass beyond this point without colliding with the Paradox, for the Unknown is known as existing, but as existing in such a way that it is beyond the capacity of reason to apprehend. 'The Reason cannot advance beyond this point, and yet it cannot refrain in its paradoxicalness from arriving at this limit and occupying itself therewith.'[12] The Unknown is the absolutely different, and therefore to man the absolute Paradox; for reason cannot conceive an absolute unlikeness to itself. If man still tries to go farther, he can only attempt to conceive the unlikeness of the Unknown by means of categories of likeness extended to infinity. In other words, he conceives God in a human image, or in images of things comprehensible to him, adding to such comprehensible qualities the category of the infinite. Thus arises human religion, and in this Kierkegaard in the main follows the exposition of natural theology given by St. Paul in Romans 1[17-32].

Where fear and wonder are preserved by the seeker without allowing the absolute unlikeness of the Godhead to be distorted and humanized by the efforts of reason, man will find God right beside him. But in that very moment, he again loses God. This is because he discovers himself as a sinner. 'No man can take note of God without becoming a sinner.'[13] Hence arises religious despair, the despair inherent in all natural religion which thus points beyond itself to the Either/Or beyond the three Stages. For all natural religion is within the sphere of an immediate and immanent relation to the Divine. Essentially it is Pantheistic, even though it may outwardly appear in the form of Polytheism, or even of Monotheism.

[11] *ST.*457.   [12] *PF.*35.   [13] *ST.*465.

Where God is not known as 'wholly-other' to man in a qualitative sense (and here Otto's conception of God as 'wholly other' fails) religion means despair. This has been well brought out by Karl Barth in his *Commentary on the Epistle to the Romans*, where religion is exposed as the highest possible corruption of man's greatest possibility. Like the boil and the ulcer, religion in this sense is the outward sign of a malignant disease within, the hidden disease of human sin. Only the radical cure proclaimed in the paradoxical Biblical revelation of the transcendent God of grace, who exists in an infinitely qualitative difference from man, can avail or solve the despair inherent in all natural religiousness. It was to expound this paradoxical religiousness of Christianity that Kierkegaard struggled throughout his life.

There are then, three Stages and an Either/Or beyond. The paradoxical nature of religious existence in this final sense lies in a special relationship of faith. This relationship of faith which is so central to Christianity is not that characteristic of all natural religion, namely a relationship of 'first immediacy'. It is on the contrary what Kierkegaard calls 'a second immediacy after reflection'. Far from being a satisfaction and heightening of human nature, it means dying to live; and its essential nature in this world is that of suffering. 'While aesthetic existence is essentially enjoyment, and ethical existence essentially struggle and victory, religious existence is essentially suffering, and that, not as a transitional moment, but as persisting.'[14] Exactly what this element of religious suffering stands for, and what it points to, is dealt with by Kierkegaard under the theme: Suffering is precisely inwardness.[15] Hence the consideration of the three Stages leads directly to Kierkegaard's difficult thesis: Truth is Subjectivity.

[14] *CUP*.256.   [15] *CUP*.256.

CHAPTER FOUR

TRUTH IS SUBJECTIVITY

The truth is precisely the venture which chooses an objective uncertainty with the passion of the infinite.
— THE CONCLUDING UNSCIENTIFIC POSTSCRIPT, 182

KIERKEGAARD'S thesis that Truth is Subjectivity is at once the most important for the understanding of his polemic against philosophical interpretations of Christianity, and at the same time the most difficult to grasp without misconception. By his approach to the problem of ultimate truth, he not only breaks away from the whole trend of European philosophy from the time of Descartes, but also from the generally accepted conception of the task of Christian theology since Melanchthon. He does this by a radical distinction between the 'knowing' Ego and the 'existing' Ego of man. Man as a thinker, as a gnosiological or epistemological Ego, is one thing. Man as a living being, as an ontological Ego, is quite another thing.

From the time of Descartes with his '*Cogito, ergo sum*', European philosophy has not only been guilty of confusing these two, but in all idealistic systems at any rate, it has substituted an abstracted transcendental Ego of thought for the individual Ego of the actually existing man. This applies especially to the great idealistic system of Hegel, with whom the term 'being' comes to mean 'being' only in an ideal sense, as thought by the thinker; whereas Kierkegaard insists that the term 'being' must only be used of the concrete factual being of individual existence in the world. The 'thing-in-itself' must not be equated with the thought or conception of it. There is a world of difference between £100 actually in one's hand, and the mere thought of £100 being in one's hand. Hegel's 'being' therefore is only 'being-in-thought' or 'thought-being', which Kierkegaard terms '*Possibility*'. 'Being-in-itself', the concrete factual being of existence, is the only 'being' which can be called '*Actuality*'.

Now what is Truth? Truth is generally defined as the conformity between being and thought. Kierkegaard is not concerned with the relative truth of Science, but with the ultimate truth of Reality and God. When the empirical cognitive spirit of man seeks to grasp this Truth, two ways of approach are possible, the one objective and the other subjective. The objective approach means starting with the objective world as given in sense impressions, comprehending this in the unity of knowledge by means of the categories of thought and conception, and then projecting it objectively in a systematized and coherent form as the Truth of reality. The objective approach thus stands for the supremacy of the intellect and mind in man. It assumes that man is primarily and fundamentally a thinking animal. It rests upon the further assumption that man as a gnosiological Ego is capable of comprehending Reality as it actually is.

Theodor Haecker, a brilliant modern thinker, marks this objective approach as the special characteristic of European philosophy; and he points out the genius of Kierkegaard in attempting to break away from it. 'He wishes to reverse the order and the procedure for both philosophy and thought. He wishes to go from the person over the things to the person, and not from the things over the person to the things.'[1] Kierkegaard starts, not from the world given in sense impressions, but from the existing Ego of the individual being. He then views the objective world from this standpoint of the ontological Ego as subject. Truth is thus to be understood as the relationship of the subject (i.e. not the thinking subject

[1] *HK*.27.

but the subjective being of man as actually existing) to Reality as apprehended in this way.

This by no means stands for what is generally called Subjectivism, i.e. the doctrine that the only reality we can know is that of our own individual consciousness. Kierkegaard was a realist, and he never fell into the subjectivism of thinking that the objective world is an illusion of the senses. For him objectivity meant the method of conceiving reality as an object of thought, or the way in which a thinker seeks to understand reality apart from his actual subjective being as an existing Ego. Such an objective approach, he maintains, leads only to a 'thought-reality', or to an 'ideal-reality' objective to man's own inner being. It leads to Possibility rather than to Actuality. Reality is not an idea to be thought, but the actual Being in which the individual participates through his nature as an ontological Ego. 'Reality can never be conceived.'[2]

THE EXISTENTIAL

What Kierkegaard means by Subjectivity is linked up with the special meaning he gives to the term *'Existence'*. This word can, of course, be used of any factual being, even of an animal or of a stone. We say: 'It exists.' But primarily, Kierkegaard uses the term in the special sense of the 'being' of man, as a quality of human being in virtue of man's special relation to the eternal and the absolute. 'To exist', in the case of man, is not just 'to be'; it means the special quality of living and acting as a man in the self-consciousness of one's eternal destiny. In his 'existence', man partakes of ultimate reality in a unique way; and therefore in relation to reality, a man must live and think 'existentially', i.e. with the full consciousness of his own individual existence. A 'thought-relationship' to reality is no relationship at all to actual reality. Man can

[2] *J*.1,054.

only relate himself to reality 'existentially', by the inner movement of his life, by the action of his will, and never by mental comprehension. An intellectual relationship to ultimate reality is impossible. An 'existential' relationship is the only one possible for man.

This problem becomes concrete when we consider the existence of God. How can we be sure that God exists? All the so-called proofs of God's existence are in their very nature based upon the possibility of an intellectual relationship to God as the Supreme Reality. Kierkegaard will therefore have nothing to do with them. He maintains that the very attempt to prove God's existence shows an utter misunderstanding of the nature of the problem. All such proofs lead ultimately only to a thought or idea of God, and never to His actual existence. They may prove His 'conceptual' existence; but there still remains the gap between what we conceive God to be and what He is actually in Himself. Kierkegaard asserts that we never actually begin to prove the existence of God unless we are already convinced of His existence. Existence is always a given *datum*. 'I do not, for example, prove that a stone exists, but that some existing thing is a stone.'[3] Existence in the sense of factual being is never subject to any logical or inferential demonstration. In this sphere, we can move only '*from*' existence and never '*toward*' it, as a conclusion.

In the attempt to know ultimate truth, the objective approach is foredoomed to failure because of the fact that as existing individuals, we are confined to space and time and therefore we can view reality only *sub specie temporis*. God alone, as the unity of Being and Thought, can view reality *sub specie aeternitatis*. When we seek to grasp reality, as Spinoza tried to do, *sub specie aeternitatis*, we grasp it only in thought, ignoring our individual selves as existing beings. The only possible approach to the whole problem

[3] *PF.*31.

is the existential or subjective approach, through the existing individual as an ontological Ego. We partake of reality, not as thinkers, but as living subjects. The moment we 'think' eternal truth and reality, that very moment we objectify it and separate it from our existing selves as subjects. But we can never grasp eternal reality by *separating* ourselves from it; we must *relate* ourselves to it. This can only be done by the subjective, existential approach.

Objectively, eternal truth can never be grasped. It always lies in uncertainty when so approached, i.e. intellectually. We can only come to know the truth by relating ourselves to it existentially in decision. The problem of God and eternal truth is a life-problem, or an existence-problem. It is never a thought-problem. Along the line of thought, no certainty can ever be reached regarding reality. Kierkegaard ultimately defines truth thus: 'An objective uncertainty held fast in an appropriation-process of the most passionate inwardness is the truth, the highest truth attainable for an existing individual.'[4] The approach through mental comprehension is essentially an impersonal approach. There is no infinite concern in it for me, for my life; it is not viewed as a problem decisive for my existence and eternal destiny. Viewed philosophically, the problem is to bring God and eternal truth to light as a task for thought. But as Kierkegaard points out: 'This is in all eternity impossible, because God is a subject, and therefore exists only for subjectivity in inwardness.'[5] The truth of God only exists for a man in so far as he relates himself to it existentially. 'God only exists for an existing man, i.e. he can only exist *in faith*. . . . When an existing individual has not got faith, God *is* not, neither does God *exist*, although understood from an eternal point of view, God is eternally.'[6]

[4] *CUP*.182.   [5] *CUP*.178.
[6] *J*.605.

THE DIALECTIC OF ETERNAL TRUTH

Eternal truth presents itself to an existing individual in time only through the form of paradox. Man himself is a divided being, who was created in God's image but who through sin has fallen away from God and is immersed in the finitude of time and space. He is compounded of time and eternity, and of freedom and necessity. Thus to man, thought and being cannot be grasped as a unity, but only in sharp contrast. As Unamuno writes: 'Rational truth and life stand in opposition to one another.'[7] Eternal truth is not in itself paradoxical, for in God thought and being are one. But by virtue of its relationship to an existing man, this truth becomes paradoxical as man seeks to grasp it. By 'paradoxical' is meant that it cannot be comprehended by man directly as a unity, but it is presented always in a contradictory form, in the tension of opposites. This further means that eternal truth can only be apprehended dialectically.

Kierkegaard develops his dialectic in immediate contrast to that of Hegel, the master dialectician of the day. Hegel's philosophical system is based upon a dialectic of development whereby the apparent contradictions on one level of 'being' are overcome in a synthesis upon a higher level of being, until the supreme height of a unified world-view of reality is reached. Kierkegaard's comment upon this kind of dialectic is that it works only so long as we confine ourselves to thought, but that it breaks down when the element of actual existence is brought in. Life or existence, in contrast to thought, is itself paradoxical, and no mere logical dialectic can resolve being and thought into a unity. A new kind of dialectic is necessary when we are dealing, as we must deal, with actual reality, and not just with the ideal-reality of thought. 'The whole of logic is quantitative or modal dialectic, since every-

[7] *The Tragic Sense of Life* (E.T.), p. 103.

was granted, he would offer up whatever first came out of the door of his house upon his return. Brutus executed with his own hands his own son according to Roman law, because he had forgotten his duty.

Now, all three of these men acted within the universal of ethics as then understood. There was an ethical 'why' to their deed which could be understood and approved by all concerned. The sacrifice of Iphigenia was the price paid for the success of the expedition. The offering up of Jephthah's daughter was the price paid for victory over the national enemy. The execution of the son of Brutus was the price paid to uphold Roman law. But Abraham's sacrifice of Isaac has no ethical 'why'. It flies in the face of all ethics. It could never have had the approval of the community. It does not in the least go according to the paradigm of the universal, though preachers have sometimes tried to draw a universal moral from the story. Kierkegaard tells of one preacher who in a sermon praised Abraham in that he loved God so much that he wanted to give to God the best he had. In the preacher's congregation there was a man who took it to heart, went home, and wanted to imitate Abraham by killing his own son. The preacher, hearing of this, went immediately to expostulate with him. But the man replied: 'This is what you yourself preached in your sermon on Sunday.'[6] No universal ethical truth or law can be drawn from Abraham's action. It can only be understood as the teleological suspension of the ethical in favour of some higher law or truth.

This of course is highly paradoxical. The absolute claim of God upon the individual may conflict with the universal obligation of ethics or of duty. In submitting to the absolute claim of God upon him, the individual isolates himself from the universal of ethical law, and relates himself absolutely to the absolute in the obedience

[6] *FT*.31.

of faith. That is to say, the personal individual relationship to God in faith may have to over-ride the universal obligation of ethical law. Love to God and obedience to God may conflict with a man's obligation to his fellowmen. It may force a man through his individual relationship to God to give to his love for his neighbour an expression contrary to his duty in the eyes of ethics. Thus this call to step out into a special individual relationship to God involves a man in religious tribulation and inward suffering.

This break with the universal, this self-isolation of the individual from the community, is the only way into the realm of the paradoxically religious, the sphere in which a man is justified by his faith. It involves an intense dialectical tension between the individual in his solidarity with the community within the ethico-religious sphere of the universal, and the individual as the individual in a particular relationship to God within the paradoxical religiousness of Biblical revelation. This is the tension of the true Christian life of faith.

Without any objective certainty, the individual must be prepared to obey God's call, no matter what the price to be paid or the suffering to be endured. He must die away from all immediacy, from all dependence upon understanding; and then venture in faith, without the least corroborative probability, upon the paradox of the special Divine relationship. It means dying to all self-reliance, whether in understanding, feeling or moral sense. 'Self-annihilation is the essential form for the God-relationship.'[7] Unless the category of the individual is stressed in this paradoxical sense, philosophy deals only in dreams, and religion with illusions.

[7] *CUP*.412.

CHAPTER SIX

REPETITION

Repetition properly so-called is recollected forwards
—REPETITION, 4

THE SAME paradox which we have seen confronting a man in his relation to God and truth also appears in his relation to eternity. He is faced with the problem: How can man in time relate himself to eternal truth? How can God in eternity reveal Himself to man in his temporal existence? We are thus called to consider what time and eternity stand for.

Kierkegaard maintains that the ordinary division of time into past, present, and future is arbitrary and artificial. When we conceive time in this way we are only spatializing it in thought. When we do this we bring time, as it were, to a standstill in order so to divide it. Actually, however, time never stands still; it is always passing. What then is time? Past time is not actual time, because it has gone by and we can only grasp it in the memory of thought by recollection. In the same way future time does not exist, for we can only think it in anticipation. The only time actual for us is the present as we exist in it. But, as we seek to grasp this present time, the 'now', we experience it only as a fleeting moment in an infinite succession. As such it is void of content, for it is gone before its content can be grasped. We are thus confronted with the paradox that time itself, whether past, present, or future, cannot be grasped by man in its actuality, but only in thought, as a mental idea. 'Precisely because every moment, like the sum of the moments, is a process, no moment is a present, and in the same sense, there is neither past, present, nor future.'[1]

What this means is that Time cannot properly be understood or become a reality to us by itself. It can only be rightly conceived and experienced dialectically, in tension with the qualitatively different 'eternity'. Eternity alone gives meaning and significance to time. To think time apart from eternity as the qualitatively different is to involve thought, as Kant has shown, in conflicting antimonies. As past, present, or future, Time can only be thought abstractly, and thus is not existentially real to us.

What then do we understand by 'eternity'? It is not time infinitely prolonged. Nor is it another kind of time in another world beyond this. Kierkegaard emphasizes that both time and eternity are realities to us, but they are qualitatively different in such a way that time has real meaning for us only when eternity impinges upon it. The eternal is the absolute, without distinction of past, present, or future. The temporal is the relative, without meaning in its fleeting succession. If then, eternal truth, the truth of the eternal reality, is to break in upon us in our temporal existence, it can be only when eternity in its infinite qualitative difference strikes down vertically upon the horizontal stream of time. The point of its impact is what Kierkegaard calls 'The Moment' or 'The Instant'.

This Moment is the *locus* of Divine revelation in the transcendent sense, as opposed to the conception of revelation as immanent and always present. Here, in the Moment, eternity touches time as a tangent touches a circle. In one sense this Moment is the present instant of time, the point on the circle of time, the 'Now', which, as we have seen, is in itself void of content, and is only the purely abstract exclusion of past and future. But in another sense the Moment is a fraction of eternity, the

[1] *CD*.77.

point of the impinging tangent. 'It is the finite reflection of eternity in time.'[2] Here alone, in the Moment where time and eternity meet, does eternal truth come into being for man in his temporal existence, as he responds to it in the act of faith.

REPETITION

In connexion with this category of the Moment, Kierkegaard develops his notion of 'Repetition', of which Dr. Lowrie says: 'No term in Sören Kierkegaard's vocabulary is more important and none so baffling,'[3] It is the title of one of Kierkegaard's early books, and it certainly will baffle anyone reading it for the first time without preparation. The deepest metaphysical disquisition is concealed in the light frivolousness of a topical newspaper column.

He contrasts Repetition with the Greek doctrine of Recollection. This doctrine stands for the position that man in his very nature partakes essentially of the eternal world, and thus has eternal truth within him. It needs but the stimulus of the teacher for the student to recollect it and to bring it forth to knowledge. Eternal truth is 'already present in embryo in the soul'. It is on this basis that Socrates argued for the immortality of the soul. Kierkegaard compares this notion with his idea of Repetition. 'Repetition is a decisive expression for what "recollection" was for the Greeks. Just as they taught that all knowledge is a recollection, so will modern philosophy teach that the whole of life is a repetition. . . . Repetition and recollection are the same movement, only in opposite directions; for what is recollected has been, is repeated backwards; whereas repetition properly so-called is recollected forward.'[4]

Eternity to the Greek was behind him, the source of his nature as man; whereas to Kierkegaard, Christianity

[2] CD.79.   [3] LR.630.   [4] R.3/4.

points to eternity ahead as the goal of man's destiny. The knowledge of eternal truth for the Christian is therefore, not by recollecting backwards, but by remembering forwards. This is possible because eternity has, what Kierkegaard calls, 'retro-active power'. When it impinges upon the time-process in the Moment, the future eternity *aeternum futurum*, i.e. eternity as it appears to us normally as ahead of us, becomes a present eternity, *aeternum praesens*, to the man of faith. Thus eternity which to us in time is still ahead and future repeats itself backwards into the human present in the Moment of revelation. Christian faith is not directed to eternity as future; that is what we call 'hope'. Christian faith is only true faith when it is directed to eternity as it becomes present, proleptically, in the Moment of impact. 'And therefore faith hopes also in this life, but, be it noted, by virtue of the absurd, not by virtue of the understanding.'[5]

Two Biblical examples of the working of Repetition are given by Kierkegaard, namely the stories of Abraham and of Job. God had promised Abraham that through Isaac his seed should become a blessing to all nations. When he was commanded to sacrifice Isaac, this seemed to the understanding to nullify the promise and to make it impossible of fulfilment. But Abraham nevertheless believed and obeyed. He had faith that somehow God would restore Isaac, not just in a future eternity, but in time and in this world. In this sense Abraham achieved repetition in relation to Isaac, for he received him back in a new relationship, as one alive from the dead. The same category applies to Job. He lost all except his life; but he continued to believe that God would justify him against the insinuations of his friends. Finally he won through to repetition by the trial of his faith; and he won back all that he had lost, though no longer in a way that he could lose it again.

[5] *J*.445.

THE PERSONAL SIGNIFICANCE OF REPETITION

The personal religious sense of Repetition in relation to time and eternity is brought out by Kierkegaard in a striking Discourse entitled: *The Joy of it—that what thou dost lose temporally, thou dost gain eternally*. Within his temporal existence, man can only lose the temporal temporally. The seriousness of life is that it is possible for man in his temporal existence to lose the eternal; and this in fact is Kierkegaard's definition of sin—in time to lose eternity. What man must strive after is to gain the eternal eternally.

Whatever loss we suffer in life, we only lose it temporally. This loss, however, may be regained eternally. That is Repetition. Christianity consists in being willing to lose the temporal completely in order thereby to gain the eternal. By renunciation of all that binds us to the temporal world, by separating ourselves in our earthly desires from all temporal possessions and relationships, we make the decisive break with the temporal. This is the prelude to the act of faith by which we gain all back again in an eternal relationship. This break with the temporal may be forced upon us by circumstances beyond our control; or it may be chosen by a definite act of surrender by the will. Then Repetition comes into play, by the re-relationship to the temporal world—no longer in a temporal sense but in an eternal manner.

Kierkegaard uses the term 'eternal' here, not in the sense of relating to a future eternity, but as a qualification of the present. When he says: 'What thou dost lose temporally, thou dost gain eternally,'[6] he does not mean: 'What thou dost lose *now*, thou dost gain *hereafter*.' He means: 'What thou dost lose *now*, in a *temporal* sense, thou dost gain *now*, in an *eternal* sense'. The temporal and the eternal are qualifications of the relationship of the self to the world and to God. The true Christian is one who breaks with the world of this temporal human life; he must die to it. But he does not flee from the world into a monastery of seclusion. He remains in the world but not of it, re-relating himself to that world in an eternal sense.

In respect of temporal loss, the sufferer must *will* decisively to let it go, understanding that it has gone only in a temporal sense. Then, by an act of faith, he must grasp hold again of what has been lost, and repeat his personal relationship to it in an eternal way. It is probable that Kierkegaard had in mind the two great losses which he himself had personally sustained, firstly that of his father by death, and secondly that of Regine by the breaking of his engagement of marriage. In a temporal sense he had lost them; but in an eternal sense, by repetition, he gained them again. His own experience shines through many of his words. 'The sufferer himself is in fact compounded of the temporal and the eternal. So when temporal existence inflicts upon him the greatest loss it is able to inflict, the question is whether . . . true to himself and to the eternal, he does not permit the loss of the temporal to become something other than it is, a temporal loss. If he does this, then the eternal in him has conquered. To let go of the temporal in such a way that it is lost temporally, to lose only temporally the lost temporal possession, is a precise indication of the presence of the eternal in the loser, it is the token that the eternal in him has conquered.'[7]

This category of Repetition is thus the religious expression of Kierkegaard's more philosophically worded dictum that we must relate ourselves absolutely to the absolute, and relatively to the relative. The absolute is the eternal; the relative is the temporal. To lose anything or to renounce anything temporally is to separate oneself from it relatively; to gain anything temporally is to gain it only relatively. Therefore the task of the Christian is to lose

[7] *Ch.D.*146.

the whole world temporally in order to gain it eternally. But to gain the whole world temporally is to lose everything eternally.

THE THEOLOGICAL SIGNIFICANCE OF REPETITION

Though Kierkegaard himself did not develop the theological significance of Repetition, his writings suggest that it may be understood in a three-fold relationship: to God; to the self; and to the world.

Firstly, in relation to God, Repetition means Justification. Man in his temporal existence has become guilty before God. He cannot justify himself; only God in His grace can do it. Driven by self-despair, and by a deep longing for eternal blessedness, deliverance from guilt and reconciliation with God, man must venture passionately upon the naked promise of God in Christ, despite its objective uncertainty. In response, God justifies him through Jesus Christ. Justification is essentially a judgement of eternity and not of time. Yet to the sinner, justification is not merely a future expectation, namely that after death, God *will* justify him or account him righteous. It is a present fact, namely, that he *is* justified here and now before God. The judgement of the eternal world upon the sinner is repeated backwards into time, so that in the Moment of faith, the eternal judgement becomes a present fact to the believer.

Secondly, in relation to the human self or soul, Repetition means Regeneration. Because of guilt before God, the natural self is condemned in the judgement of eternity to death. In the act of faith in Christ the sinner anticipates this judgement of eternity; he reckons himself dead in trespasses and sins through self-crucifixion with Christ. Only then does the possibility of Regeneration and newness of life arise. This new life in Christ is a repetition, a re-creation, under a new possibility, namely, resurrection from the dead. It is the life of eternity repeated backwards into time. It is what the New Testament calls 'eternal life', which the believer enjoys here and now within time. It is what David Swenson, a keen Kierkegaardian student calls 'the restoration of the personal consciousness to its normal integrity', i.e. to what God intended it to be.

Thirdly, in relation to the world, Repetition means the Kingdom of God. In relation to human history it stands for the restoration of the Age of sinlessness and deathlessness, foretold by the prophets. This does not mean an Age of life as it was before the Fall of man into sin, but human life under a new qualification, namely, that the powers of evil are for ever overthrown and destroyed. In Christ that new Age has come—the eternal kingdom of God. This kingdom is not just the reign of God in a future eternity beyond death. It is here and now, coming into existence for the believer in the Moment of faith. The kingdom of God which in itself is ahead of us beyond death is repeated backwards from eternity into time in the coming of Christ. The old world, this present age of sin and death, still continues; but in Christ it is essentially negated and overcome. The true life of the believer is thus lived in the power of the Age-to-come. He has been 'translated' into the Kingdom of Christ. The world has no more power or authority over him; he is a citizen of heaven. He is crucified and dead, not only to self, but also to the world. Here and now he is alive for ever more in the blessedness of the Kingdom of God.

God is the absolute, and that time cannot essentially differentiate the absolute, otherwise it would be reduced to a relative. The God-man stands for the absolute in the relative. Christ is historical fact *and* eternal fact. Historically, only His own generation in Palestine was contemporaneous with Him. To them He appeared as a man and claimed to be God. Humanly speaking, everything seemed against that claim. There was nothing at all to mark Him out as other than a man amongst men. Thus His contemporaries were confronted with the paradox of His being, face to face. How then does it fare with succeeding generations? If the only real relationship, i.e. a relationship of existence and not merely in thought, is the contemporaneous one, how can the man of today relate himself to the God-man who appeared nineteen centuries ago? A mere thought-relationship in historical memory is utterly ineffective for man's predicament. A relationship of contemporaneousness is absolutely essential. 'No relationship with the God-man is possible except by beginning with the situation of contemporaneousness.'[5]

Kierkegaard answers this point with his doctrine of the Eternal Contemporaneousness of the God-man. Christ's life on earth is an historical fact. But it is more: it is an eternal event, the manifestation of the absolute eternal in relative time. If, as Christ claims, His life on earth provides the basis for man's blessedness in eternity, then the necessary relationship between the believer and Christ cannot be merely an historical one. In that sense the contemporary of Christ in Palestine had no advantage over succeeding generations. Since Christ as the God-man is the eternal manifestation of the absolute, Christ is contemporaneous with every historical age. 'For in relation to the absolute there is only one tense: the present. For him who is not contemporary with the absolute—for him it has no existence.'[6]

[5] *TR.*84. [6] *TR.*67.

Christ's earthly life thus possesses the unique quality of being contemporaneous with every age, by virtue of His nature as the absolute eternal. The paradox in which He presents Himself to us as the God-man is equally real to every generation. It is a living, contemporaneous paradox, by which Christ comes to man in the Moment of revelation. Just as colours exist for sight, and sounds for hearing, so the absolute paradox exists only for faith. Christ's eternal contemporaneousness is a contingent contemporaneousness, contingent upon the response of faith on the part of man. Though it is nineteen hundred years since Christ walked this earth His life is not a bygone event like other historical happenings to be grasped only in memory. 'No, His presence here on earth never becomes a bygone event . . . in case faith is to be found on earth. . . . So long as there is a believer, such a one must, in order to become such, have been and as a believer must continue to be just as contemporary with His presence on earth as were those first contemporaries. This contemporaneousness is the condition of faith, and more closely defined, it is faith.'[7]

No other event of history can become contemporaneous to a man of today. This is one of the radically distinguishing marks of Christianity. Only when Christ becomes contemporaneous with a man can that man truly make the venture of faith in Him. 'Only the contemporary is reality for me. . . . And thus every man can be contemporary only with the age in which he lives—and then with one thing more: with Christ's life on earth; for Christ's life on earth, sacred history, stands for itself alone outside history.'[8] By 'sacred history' Kierkegaard does not mean religious history in general, or the history of religious movements. He means those events in history which as events of special Divine revelation, partake also of the quality of the eternal. Sacred history is composed of those events in which the transcendent world of God impinges upon the world of man, and of which the Bible is the human record. This sacred history centres in the events of Christ's appearance upon earth, His death, and His resurrection. It is this sacred history which is the vehicle of Divine revelation and which accompanies time and human history in such a way as to be capable of becoming contemporaneous with the individual of any age in the Moment of faith. 'Christ's life on earth is not a past event. . . . His earthly life accompanies the race, and accompanies every generation in particular, as the eternal history. His earthly life possesses the eternal contemporaneousness.'[9]

This does not mean that the passing of the centuries can make it any clearer who Christ was, or that it can in any way lessen the absoluteness of the paradox of the God-man for us. All such arguments, that time has shown the truth of Christ's claim to be God (what Kierkegaard calls 'the proof of the centuries') are utterly fallacious. From world history, from ecclesiastical history, from missionary history, or from any other kind of human history, we can in the strict sense learn nothing of the secret of Christ. 'He is the paradox, the object of faith, existing only for faith. But all historical communication is communication of "knowledge"; hence from history one can learn nothing about Christ.'[10]

This absolute paradox of the God-man lies in the unity of God and an individual man. It is the revelation of eternal truth in time. It is the paradox which neither thought nor reason can grasp, and yet which proclaims itself as the only basis for man's eternal blessedness. It faces every generation with the same demand. Its objective uncertainty, and the Divine elusiveness which refuses any directly comprehensible revelation, potentiates the

[9] *TR*.68. [10] *TR*.28.

inward passion by which man must seek to relate himself to it. It is this inward passion, this fear and trembling, which corresponds to the paradox of divine revelation in Christ. For faith is such a passion; and without faith, there is no salvation.

CHAPTER EIGHT

THE SIGN OF CONTRADICTION

The God-man is the sign of contradiction
—TRAINING IN CHRISTIANITY, 126

THE NATURE of the paradox involved in the concept of the God-man makes explicit the principle that there can be no direct communication of eternal truth to man. By the very nature of the human situation in relation to God, any revelation of eternal truth must be indirect. No direct knowledge or understanding of God is possible. Christian revelation stands for the principle that what is revealed is the Revealer himself, and not just some truth about him. Christ's revelation is not His teaching in any objective sense. Christ is Divine revelation in the fact that He exists in His teaching, and that the teaching has significance only in direct reference to Him who taught.

Since the very nature of the paradox of revelation thus precludes any form of direct communication, it can be manifested to man in his temporal existence only in the form of a sign. What is a sign? 'A sign is the negation of immediacy, or a second state of being differing from the first.'[1] By 'immediacy', Kierkegaard means that which is directly apprehended by the senses, in contrast with a notion which is derived from reflection. A sign therefore is something which in its immediacy points onward to something else which is different. A white flag is a sign. In itself, i.e. in its immediacy, it is only a piece of white cloth. But, as a sign, it stands for the desire of the bearer to cease hostilities.

[1] *TR*.124.

Strictly speaking, a sign is only a sign to one who comes to know what it signifies, i.e. to one who is able to reflect on it and understand its meaning. Kierkegaard refers to the classical story of how the son of Tarquin after the capture of Gabies sent a messenger to his father to ask what he should do next. Secrecy was essential. So Tarquin took the messenger into his garden, struck off the tops of the tallest poppies, and sent the messenger back to his son. What the father meant was understood by the son but not by the messenger; for the son immediately executed the chief men of Gabies. The action of Tarquin was a sign. Such a sign becomes necessary when there can be no direct communication. A ship in distress thus flies its flag upside down.

Now, Christ, the God-man, is a sign. In His immediacy, He is a man; but at the same time, He claims to be God. His divinity cannot be directly communicated as know-ledge; it can only be apprehended through the sign of His humanity. Christ, however, is not a sign in the sense of a symbol which can be understood directly by anyone after a little reflection. As the absolute paradox to man, He is what Kierkegaard calls 'a sign of contradic-tion'. This term is taken from Luke 2[34]: 'Behold, this child is set . . . for a sign which shall be spoken against.'[2]

A sign of contradiction is one which as a sign is am-biguous, a unity of two opposites or contradictories. It thus signifies two possible alternative senses, each of which is contrary to the other. 'A sign of contradiction is one which draws attention to itself, and then, when attention is fixed upon it, shows that it contains a contradiction.'[3] To take another illustration from ancient Roman legends, it is like when the two sons of Tarquin with their cousin, Lucius Brutus, went to the oracle at Delphi to inquire which of them should reign after Tarquin. The priestess

[2] *Greek—seemeion antilegomenon.*   [3] *TR.*125.

No mere superlative of the human can ever make the Divine.

Thus, there was no direct evidence of Christ's Divinity for His contemporaries; nor is there any proof of the truth of His claim for the acceptance of succeeding generations. Christ's incognito was an absolute one; and this is the distinguishing mark of His nature as Divine revelation. Faced with the paradox of Christ's claim to be God, the individual cannot resolve it by thought or reason. He is forced to choose by an act of will. 'If he really were the Son of God, the proof would be ridiculous, just as ridiculous as though a man were to prove his own existence, since in this case Christ's existence and His divinity are the same.'[6]

THE CHOICE—FAITH OR OFFENCE

In relation to Christ as the sign of contradiction in His impenetrable incognito, man is forced to stand in a situation of choice and decision. By his individual choice every man reveals what sort of a man he is. 'The contradiction puts before him a choice, and while he is choosing, he himself is revealed.'[7] Christ stands before a man as a kind of mirror, challenging him to faith or offence. It is a challenge, not just to his thought, but to his very self as an existing being. From the point of view of thought and understanding alone, Christ of necessity becomes offence, for He is the absolute paradox.

Kierkegaard makes much of this category of 'offence'. 'Just as the concept "faith" is a highly characteristic note of Christianity, so also is "offence" a highly characteristic note of Christianity and stands in close relation to faith. The possibility of offence is the crossways, or it is like standing at the crossways. From the possibility of offence a man turns either to offence or to faith.'[8] In the situation of contemporaneousness, the offence of Christ immediately becomes apparent. He draws attention to His claim by His miracles; but He affords no direct proof or evidence of the truth of His claim. In the situation of contemporaneousness, miracles are certainly not conclusive. You are faced with a man who claims to be God. If you do not believe His claim the miracle can be explained away. If you already accept His claim the miracle as proof becomes superfluous. Therefore in the situation of contemporaneousness the miracle proves nothing; it simply draws attention, so that one comes face to face with the paradox of the nature of the miracle-worker.

The Christian category of Offence has two main forms: firstly, that of Loftiness, in that an ordinary man claims to be God; secondly, that of Lowliness, in that God suffers as a lowly man. It should particularly be noted that Offence has to do directly with the person of Christ Himself, and not with His teaching or with the religious principles He advocated. 'The God-man is the paradox, absolutely the paradox; hence it is quite clear that the understanding must come to a standstill before it. If a man does not notice the offence which has to do with loftiness, he will on the other hand discover that which has to do with lowliness.'[9] There can be no true faith except through the possibility of offence. The nature of this possibility of offence is the same for us as for Christ's own contemporaries, for it is related to human existence and not just to human thought. Faith is not a matter of understanding, but related to an act of the will in the presence of the Divine revelation in Christ. It is a revelation of existence and not of knowledge. 'Comprehension is coterminous with man's relation to the human, but faith is man's relation to the divine.'[10] Where comprehension is predominant we are still in the realm of natural human religion.

[9] *TR*.85.   [10] *SD*.154.

The category of Offence is therefore integral to Christianity. 'Blessed is he whosoever shall not be offended in me.'[11] The lack of emphasis upon this category in modern philosophical theology is the measure of its distance from the outlook of the New Testament. When Christianity loses its power to offend it has lost its power to save. When 'the offence of the cross' has ceased, Christianity no longer exists. To Kierkegaard the Gospel comes as an absolute imperative. 'Thou *shalt* believe.' On his way from Egypt to France in 1799, Napoleon is reported to have said: 'The Religion of Jesus is a threat; that of Mohammed a promise.' There is some true insight in this remark, though it is not the whole truth. So long as the Gospel is presented as a polite invitation or suggestion it will meet generally with polite indifference. But the New Testament presents the Gospel as a royal imperative. 'It says to every individual, "Thou shalt believe", i.e. thou shalt either be offended or thou shalt believe.'[12]

To refuse to make any decision is no escape from the dilemma, for the very refusal to choose is itself rebellion against God and thus offence. No man can escape the choice when Christianity is rightly presented. When it is set forth as a direct communication of the knowledge of eternal truth one may or may not hold an opinion about it. Objectively as a spectator one has calmly to consider the arguments for and against it. But this is to abolish the possibility of offence. 'Take away the possibility of offence, as they have done in Christendom, and the whole of Christianity is direct communication; and then Christianity is done away with, for it has become an easy thing, a superficial something which neither wounds nor heals profoundly enough.'[13] If there is no possibility of offence, there is no possibility of faith. Christ presents the double possibility to us because He is the absolute

<hr>

[11] Matthew 11⁷.   [12] *SD*.200.   [13] *TR*.139.

paradox and the sign of contradiction. Only by our choice of faith can our existence be transformed. We must choose whether to sacrifice time for eternity, or eternity for time. Are we vitally concerned only with thought, or with our very existence?

'fear and trembling'; and the only kind of doubt for which there is room in Christianity is the subjective doubt whether one has really made the decisive venture. This negates also that kind of childish faith of immediacy, which is not Christian faith but only simple credulity. Faith is against the understanding, and always 'in virtue of the absurd'. Far from being the easy, simple, natural thing which it is pictured to be by some Christian preachers, the act of true Christian faith by which sin is overcome and the soul healed, is the most difficult task in the whole realm of human effort. Is this not what Dostoevsky means when he testifies: 'It is not as a child that I believe and confess Jesus Christ. My "hosanna" is born of a furnace of doubt.'[8]

Faith exists in tension with doubt, but only in the sense that there is doubt of one's personal relationship to Christ. 'Lord, I believe; help thou mine unbelief.'[9] It is in this sense that we must take the words of Miguel de Unamuno: 'Only those who doubt can truly believe; those who neither doubt nor are tempted contrary to their faith, do not in truth believe.'

Faith is indeed a struggle of the heart against the head, of the vital impulse of existence against the cold calculations of the reason. Because of the corruption caused by sin, the faith-relationship to God in Christ means 'dying to live', the crucifixion of the self, the denial and negation of the natural man, in order that the new man, created anew in Christ, may arise in the power of the resurrection as 'spirit'. In this understanding of the Gospel, there is no room for doubt, but only for faith.

DESPAIR

The radical disease of humanity, of which doubt is only an outward symptom, is Despair. Despair is the 'sickness

---

[8] *Nicolas Berdyaev*, Evgueny Lampert, p. 96.   [9] Mark 9²⁴.

unto death' from which the whole of humanity suffers, and from which it can only be cured by a right self-diagnosis. It is a disease relating to the individual existence in its deepest roots. 'Doubt is a despair of thought; despair is a doubt of the personality.'[10] Kierkegaard's analysis of despair is a great contribution to Christian theology and to the understanding of human life. Emil Brunner writes: 'It was no mere whim of Kierkegaard when he undertook to try to represent the whole of human life—in so far as it is not in "faith"—as despairing, and its phenomena as countless variations on the one theme of despair; and the book in which he does so, has become one of the finest of his writings.'[11]

The first part of this book (*Sickness unto Death*) is devoted to a psychological analysis of the human heart and of human existence in order to show that the whole of it is despair. The various forms of despair are described. No man can escape, for all men are seen to be essentially in a state of despair who have not won through to Christian faith. The second part of the book elaborates the thesis that despair is sin, and that sin is essentially 'before God'. The book is not easy reading because of its abstract definitions, and the exact connotation of the terms need to be clearly grasped.

Just as the aesthetical man is counselled by the Judge, in *Either/Or*, to choose despair in order to enter the ethico-religious sphere of existence, so the ethico-religious man in his dilemma of personal guilt must take the plunge of total despair in order to reach forward to the paradoxical religiousness of Christianity. In the Kierkegaardian sense, despair is not despair over *something*, but despair of *oneself*. It is a sickness of the spirit which is the more potentiated the farther one advances into existence in relation to God. It is a fever of the soul, rising and falling, only to rise again until it breaks finally in the act of Christian faith.

[10] *E/O.*2/178.   [11] *Man in Revolt* (E.T.), p. 201.

The deadliness of the sickness lies in the fact that it is not usually recognized by the patient himself. Until he does, there is no hope of a cure. No man is free from this universal sickness of despair. 'There lives not one single man who after all is not to some extent in despair, in whose inmost parts there does not dwell a disquietude, a perturbation, a discord, an anxious dread of an unknown something, or of a something he does not even dare to make acquaintance with, dread of a possibility of life, or dread of himself.'[12]

Being a category of the spirit, despair must be viewed with a qualitative dialectic. Despair is a disrelationship in the synthesis of the spirit in man. The self only overcomes despair when, having despaired infinitely, it becomes grounded transparently in God through faith. The depth of despair depends upon the quality of the consciousness of self. In extreme forms, despair may end in defiance, especially where there is a strong consciousness of the infinity of the self.

All despair is sin, because it is essentially a refusal to be the self which God intends one to be. 'Sin is this: before God, or with the conception of God, to be in despair at not willing to be oneself, or in despair at willing to be oneself. Thus sin is potentiated weakness, or potentiated defiance; sin is the potentiation of despair.'[13] The self can only be a true human self, i.e. spirit, by the rerelation to God in His qualitative difference from man. To some extent despair can be recognized wherever there is a consciousness of something eternal and infinite in the human self. But what makes despair sin in the deepest sense, is that it becomes despair before God. Thus sin is recognized as sin in the real sense only in Christendom. In Paganism the measure of sin is the human self, or the self in relation to God in immanence. Sin is a determinant of spirit, but spirit in the true sense is not and cannot be present in Paganism. 'Neither paganism nor the natural man knows what sin is.'[14]

FREEDOM AND DIVINE GOVERNANCE

Man is a synthesis not only of the finite and the infinite, and of the temporal and the eternal; but also of necessity and freedom. Kierkegaard was a passionate advocate of man's individual freedom. Knowing full well that the problem of human freedom can only be dealt with by a qualitative dialectic, he rejects the notion of a completely free, undetermined human will; and just as decisively, he rejects orthodox predestination or determinism.

On the one hand, Christian faith is a gift of the Holy Spirit. It is not a natural capacity of man; it is a determination of man by God in the Moment of revelation. On the other hand, it is equally an act of human decision, a choice and a leap, which man makes by an act of will. Thus the venture of faith in its totality corresponds to the paradox of its object, the God-man, Jesus Christ. The primal act of sin is likewise an act of freedom, and yet at the same time sin is universal.

In what sense therefore is a man free, that is, free to sin and free to believe? Whatever we may say about the fact that all men born into this world become sinners, Christianity posits a freedom to believe which is paradoxically a freedom to which man must in some way be compelled. The call of the Gospel comes to a man with the proclamation that his eternal blessedness depends upon a right relationship of faith to Christ. In a very real sense he is free to make the decision, that is, if the passion of his inwardness is sufficiently strong to force him to seize hold of the paradoxical form in which the object of faith is presented to him. It is the man he is which determines the choice he makes. In cold rational objectivity,

[14] *SD*.144.

he cannot make a real choice. There is no ultimate knowledge of God revealed prior to or apart from the act of faith itself. 'Christianity says to a man: you shall choose the one essential thing, but in such a way that there is no question of a choice. . . . The very fact that in this sense there is no choice, expresses the tremendous passion or intensity with which it must be chosen.'[15]

Man thus has formal freedom but not material freedom. Freedom in faith is a possibility only in God. 'Freedom only exists because the same moment it exists it rushes with infinite speed to bind itself unconditionally.'[16] In indecision, and in the search for some objective probability, man is just juggling with a phantom of freedom. Only in the Moment, in the instant of the revelation of God's presence, is freedom in faith possible. 'The most tremendous thing which has been granted to man is: the choice, freedom. If you desire to save it and preserve it, there is only one way; in the very same second, unconditionally and in complete resignation, to give it back to God and yourself with it.'[17]

Kierkegaard further develops his conception of the dialectical freedom of the Christian man, under the category of Divine Governance. This is not what we generally call Providence, that is, the divine help and guidance which 'provides'. Divine Governance is the power of God which rules and over-rules the events and circumstances of a man's life toward a definite goal. It has nothing to do with any inward mystical guidance. It is a compelling Governance from outside, which hedges a man along a divinely-chosen path once that man has surrendered himself to God in faith.

Kierkegaard came to see this Divine Governance at work in the order and development of his own literary labours. In a more general way he came to recognize it also in his upbringing in relationship to his father, in

[15] J.1051.   [16] J.1051.   [17] J.1051.

the breaking of his engagement of marriage to Regine Olsen, and in his conflict with the *Corsair*. In the spiritual darkness of his mind at the time he struggled against what seemed to him to be a cruel fate; but, later, he came to realize the wisdom and the grace of the Divine Governance by which the abnormal experiences and sufferings of his life were directed toward his 'Training in Christianity'.

There is a sense in which God leaves a man free, and only pleads with him persuasively without coercion, inward or outward. But when a man ventures out deeply into the Christian life, willing to relate himself absolutely to the absolute, he soon comes to find his need of something more than his own strength. He needs God to compel him, and he even prays for God to compel him through events and situations beyond his control. Kierkegaard had a strong sense of being a life-long penitent. He felt his guilt before God to such an extent that he acknowledged that his life was forfeited to God and that he must acquiesce in any measures which God might take with him.

Kierkegaard pictures a man riding a frightened horse, which he deliberately spurs forward against the very object of its fear. Only in this way can the horse be made to overcome its fear. In the same way God uses His compelling Governance upon us, once we have surrendered ourselves into His hands. Even though we cannot fully understand, and even though we shrink from the sufferings involved, we trust and know that God's purpose is always one of love.

CHAPTER TEN

A DEAD MAN SPEAKS

My life will cry out after my death—THE JOURNALS, 1090

WE HAVE already noted that Kierkegaard had a strong conviction that his life's work was largely one for posterity, and that he was not likely to be properly understood in his own day. Though *Either/Or* and some of his other more aesthetical and ethical books were fairly widely read in Denmark, his larger philosophical work, *The Concluding Unscientific Postscript*, is said to have sold only sixty copies during his lifetime. His more religious books, such as *The Works of Love* and *Christian Discourses*, were appreciated, but only in a small circle. His more polemical books, such as *Training in Christianity* and *For Self-Examination*, met with a poor reception at the time, since they attacked not only the State Church but also questioned the general nature of Christianity as propounded in Protestantism. But he was not discouraged; time would reveal the value of his work. 'I belong to history, knowing assuredly that I shall find a place there, and what place it will be.'[1]

After his death his name gradually became known in Germany and in German-speaking countries through translations of some of his books in that language. Certain Danish scholars also began the task of collating and publishing critical editions of all his works and papers. But, amidst the prevailing ethical idealism of the late nineteenth century, Kierkegaard's work came at first as a disturbing factor, and thus had little influence. In fact, it was not until the beginning of the twentieth century that Kierkegaard's claim to greatness was seriously put

[1] *PV*.98.

forward. This claim has been substantiated through the work of two noted philosophers and of two leading theologians. These are Martin Heidegger and Karl Jaspers on the one hand, and Karl Barth and Emil Brunner on the other. Through their writings and through that of other leading thinkers, the name of Kierkegaard has come to be placed high up in the list of great Christian writers of all ages. Werner Brock gives his opinion thus: 'I am inclined to believe that, if the history of the philosophy of Christianity were to be written, his interpretation would be ranked among the few great efforts to conceive Christianity as it originally was, an attempt made formerly by Augustine and Luther.'[2]

Heidegger and Jaspers are the leaders of a movement of thought on the Continent which has been called 'Existential Philosophy'. This undoubtedly takes its rise from Kierkegaard's stress upon the vital importance of the 'existential' in opposition to the abstract idealism of the Hegelian type of philosophy. In contrast to the conception of philosophy as the exposition of a logically consistent world-view of reality in a system of thought, Existential Philosophy takes the actual concrete existence of the individual man as the basis of its approach to reality. In itself, this Existential Philosophy is not definitely a religious philosophy, but it does hold fast to the basic importance of the actual existence of the individual to a right approach to philosophical understanding.

Barth and Brunner are the leaders of the important religious movement known as 'The Theology of Crisis', or more generally in some circles as 'Neo-Orthodoxy'. Barth, in his epoch-making *Commentary on the Epistle to the Romans* (1918) acknowledges his debt to the Dane in unmistakable terms by frequent references and quotations. In Barth's lectures published in English under the title *The Word of God and the Word of Man*, the Swiss theologian

[2] *Contemporary German Philosophy*, p. 76.

claims that his own line of thought runs through Kierke-gaard and Luther to Jeremiah. In his *Dogmatik* also, Barth makes frequent references to Kierkegaard. Though in his pamphlet *Nein! Antwort an Emil Brunner*, Barth has sharply distinguished his own view-point in some respects from that of Kierkegaard, especially upon the problem of the *analogia entis*, the fact remains that what distinguishes Barth from the older Liberal theologians is the Kierke-gaardian stress upon the infinite qualitative difference between God and man, and between time and eternity. Brunner in the same way acknowledges his great debt to Kierkegaard, frequently quoting with approval from his writings, and holding many of his books in the highest esteem for their Christian insight.

Many of the leading and most-read Christian thinkers of the present day owe much, directly or indirectly, to Kierkegaard and his interpretation of Christianity. We may mention Richard Niebuhr and Nicolas Berdyaev, Buber and Baillie, Mackay and Mackintosh, Camfield and Whale, and many others. But the same is true on the Continent. Evgueny Lampert, in a recent book on *Nicolas Berdyaev*,[3] states: 'The mind of Europe is under the sway of the melancholy, obscure, and tragic Kierkegaard.' In the critical disturbing days after the first World War, and now again after the second World War, Kierkegaard's radical criticism of the super-ficial optimism of Protestant Christendom is finding a ready response and quickened understanding amongst those who are seeking light in the midst of a growing darkness.

In the English-speaking world, little was known of Kierkegaard until Karl Barth's works became available and provided the stimulus to the study of the Danish thinker. Previous references to Kierkegaard are few. In Martensen's *Christian Ethics* (translated into English in

[3] Page 60.

1873) there is a certain general criticism of Kierkegaard from the standpoint of ethical idealism. There was also a pamphlet printed about Kierkegaard in Cambridge in 1908. Baron Friedrich von Hügel mentions him in *The Mystical Element of Religion* (1909) and Forsyth shows some acquaintance with him and calls Kierkegaard 'that Pascal of the North'.[4] There is also an article on Kierkegaard in Hastings' *Encyclopædia of Religion and Ethics* by Dr. A. Grieve.

But it was not until 1935 that there appeared almost simultaneously two books in English about Kierkegaard, one by E. L. Allen: *Kierkegaard, His Life and Thought*; and another by John A. Bain: *Sören Kierkegaard, His Life and Religious Teaching*. These were followed in 1936 by a translation of two essays on *Kierkegaard* by Theodor Haecker. Then came the massive and authoritative life of *Kierkegaard* by Dr. Walter Lowrie (1938). A *Shorter Life* followed in 1945. In the meantime, nearly the whole of the important works of Kierkegaard had been translated into English, including *The Journals*, thus affording the English student the material for direct study of Kierkegaard's ideas.

Curiously enough, the appreciation of Kierkegaard is not confined to Protestant circles. A number of Catholic writers have shown an interest in him in a way unusual for them. Przywara, a brilliant Jesuit writer, made a special study of Kierkegaard which he published in German under the title: *Das Geheimnis Kierkegaards* (1929). Theodor Haecker, again, has translated some of Kierkegaard's works and has lectured on his ideas. He describes the Dane as 'a great and incomparable genius'.[5] We should further note the work of the great Spanish philosopher, Don Miguel de Unamuno, himself a Catholic, who testifies of his appreciation of Kierkegaard in saying: 'I learned the language [Danish] in order to read Ibsen, but

---

[4] *The Principle of Authority*, p. 79.   [5] *HK*.17.

CHAPTER ELEVEN

THE THEOLOGY OF THE UNCONDITIONAL

People have lost the conception of the absolute requirement
—FOR SELF-EXAMINATION, 168

IN MANY ways, Kierkegaard approaches the theological problem differently from most other Protestant theologians. Down through the ages Christian theology has concerned itself in the main with the question: 'What is Christianity? Is it true?' Theology has understood its task to be the exposition of eternal truth in the light of the Christian revelation. It sets forth to answer the question: 'What is the content of the Christian Faith? What is it that a man has to believe to be a Christian?'

Kierkegaard approaches the essential task of Christian theology from quite a different angle, corresponding to his important distinction between the epistemological (gnosiological) Ego and the existential (ontological) Ego. The main question is framed by him thus: 'What does it mean for me to become a Christian?' He thus shifts the emphasis from the *What* of belief to the *How* of faith. He sets forth Christianity as a communication of existence, i.e. as a relationship of the existential Ego to Christ. He opposes the common conception of Christian theology that Christianity is a communication of knowledge, i.e. a relationship of the epistemological Ego to Christian revelation.

Kierkegaard maintains that in Christianity, if the *How* of faith, the *fides qua creditur*, is rightly grasped and the leap of faith is rightly made, then the *What* of belief, the *fides quae creditur*, is in essence given with it. The two correspond exactly, fitting together like a hand in a skin-tight glove. But, if we start with the *What* of belief, and concentrate on understanding the true doctrines of Christianity, then the leap of true faith can never be rightly made. For understanding is always in the nature of a parenthesis; it is never completed. Any venture of faith that is made is then only provisional; and a provisional leap of faith is of necessity relative and never absolute. It is always like a man swimming—with one foot on the bottom.

Reflection upon Christian doctrine can never enable a man to become a Christian. 'One does not reflect oneself into being a Christian, but out of another thing in order to become a Christian.'[1] In the sphere of immediacy without reflection, to become a Christian is a perfectly straightforward thing. The simple unreflective man can make the movement of faith without the agonizing struggle that awaits the intellectual man. For the latter, reflection is necessary, but not in order to become a Christian. Rather, the intellectual man has to reflect himself out of any intellectual relationship and discover that Christianity is not a communication of knowledge to be understood, but a communication of existence which has to be grasped by the leap of faith which is beyond comprehension and heterogeneous from reason.

Christianity therefore is essentially a personal and individual relationship of faith to Christ as the absolute paradox. It is Kierkegaard's stress upon the unique nature of the paradoxical religiousness peculiar to Christianity which marks him out so distinctively from other theologians of the nineteenth century. As we have seen, Kierkegaard admits and indeed emphasizes the natural religiousness of man as man; but he radically distinguishes Christian religiousness from this, and he denies that Christianity is in any way a fulfilment, enhancement, improvement or perfection of religion in itself. In natural religion, i.e. the religion of immediacy which is based upon a relationship to the Divine as immanent in all Creation and especially in man, faith is a natural capacity

[1] *PV*.96.

of man as man. Kierkegaard is here thinking not only of what we usually call heathen or pagan religions, but also of forms of religion which are called Christian and yet which work only in the categories of natural religion. 'What does it mean that all these thousands and thousands call themselves Christians as a matter of course? These many, many men of whom the greater part, as far as one can judge, live in categories quite foreign to Christianity?'[2]

Kierkegaard is not here concerned with the fact that many people do not live up to the standard of Christian morality. His criticism is quite different. He is concerned with what Christian people themselves hold to be the Christian standard and the Christian ideal of life. He argues that in Christendom, the religious ideal held by most people is simply the ideal of natural religion under a Christian name. Many Christians, even devout Church members, live in aesthetical, or at the most, ethico-religious categories belonging to natural religion. This is what he calls Religiousness A. This natural religiousness, whether in Christendom or in Paganism, always presumes a direct relationship to the Divine; it assumes a kinship or continuity between humanity and divinity. Christianity or Religiousness B, on the other hand, stands for the infinitely qualitative difference between God and man, and between eternity and time, in such a way that Christian revelation can only come in the form of an absolute paradox to man, and as an offence to his reason. To the natural man, religiousness means blessedness and prosperity and divine help in time of need. But to the Christian who has entered into the paradoxical religiousness of Christianity, religiousness means suffering, worldly loss, a dying to self and to the world. 'Whom God blesses in a religious sense, He *eo ipso* curses in a worldly sense.'[3]

Just as the controls of an aeroplane change their function when the plane is turning at an angle over forty-five degrees, so the meaning of the categories changes when we pass from Religiousness A to Religiousness B. Natural religion moves in the categories of the relative and the conditional; Christianity moves in the categories of the absolute and the unconditional.

The force of the absolute and the unconditional in religion can only be felt and appreciated by the individual as an individual, and never by the group or the community as a whole. Natural religion is always essentially group religion, even though practised by the individual. Christianity is essentially individual religion, even though practised within the group. But, in considering Kierkegaard's stress upon the individual, we must be careful not to confuse it with secular Individualism. Kierkegaard is not concerned with the individual in and by himself, but only with the individual in relationship to God. His is a religious individualism. As Stewart Means points out: 'At its roots, religion is primarily individual, that is, it is a personal relation, essentially a matter between God and the soul of man. Its social aspects are . . . mainly derivative and not primary.'[4] Whitehead echoes the same thought in his oft-quoted remark: 'Religion is what the individual does with his solitariness.'[5] All students of Buber's 'I and Thou' will recognize the stress laid by him also on the category of the individual in his relationships. Buber has been stimulated by Kierkegaard's thought upon this subject, and both stress what we may call Relational Individualism. Christian faith is a *meeting* (not an understanding) where the 'wholly-other', transcendent God becomes a present, unutterably near 'Thou' to me in my individual consciousness as 'I'. Only in this way does a sense of the Divine unconditional pierce into the heart of man.

Kierkegaard has been accused, especially by Bishop Martensen, of having no sense of the Church. 'Through-

[4] *Faith*, p. 327.   [5] *Religion in the Making*, p. 16.

out the whole diffuse literature we look in vain for the idea of the Church.'[6] This is only partly true. We can agree with Martensen that the category of the Church cannot possibly be left out in any consideration of Christian theology. The Church is not a mere fortuitous collection of individual Christians. In a very real sense, it is the body of Christ, an organic unity of its members in Christ the Head. But in the world, the visible Church is only a relative and not an unconditional. Martensen is on very debatable ground when he argues that the Church stands for the synthesis of individualism and collectivism, and that the Christian community has equal ontological reality with the individual in relation to God.

Kierkegaard would argue that the individual relationship to God is primary, and that there can be no question at all of any Church without the prior postulation of individual Christians. The Church exists for the individual and not the individual for the Church. The individual is not a means to an end, but the Church is. It is the individual who is, by reason of his eternal destiny, related in possibility to the unconditional.

Kierkegaard queries whether there is any longer in the world a Church in the New Testament sense. What he saw around him was a Triumphant Church, a Church which had coalesced with the State, a Church which boasted of its conquest of the world without realizing that in conquering, it had itself been conquered from within. The New Testament Church is a Militant Church, a company of men and women who had renounced the world and who were ready at all times to suffer for the doctrine they believed. They were a body of witnesses to the truth who lived as dead to the world, crucified with Christ. They were scorned and hated by the world.

But in Christendom, Kierkegaard only saw a monstrous illusion, a mass of nominal Christians, who however good

[6] *Christian Ethics* (E.T.), p. 228.

and respectable they might appear, lived in the categories of natural religion. Only by breaking up this mass into separate individuals could the message of the Gospel come home personally to them. In a group, even in a Church, the sense of individual responsibility to God is fatally weakened. There is and can be no sense of the unconditional so long as the individual is absorbed in the group. He must be separated, isolated before God, if ever the word of God in its personal address is to reach him.

Kierkegaard is undoubtedly the forerunner of what is now often called 'The Theology of the Word of God'. He set himself to present the unconditional demand of the Word of God upon men, to awaken unrest in men's hearts by exposing the relativity and instability of any relationship to God which is only 'to a certain extent'. He poured his scorn upon those who took God for granted, and who conceived eternal life and salvation as the natural inheritance of all those born in Christendom. With all the skill of his poetic pen he tried to raise the ideal of what is demanded of a Christian. With him it was not so much a question of raising the actual nearer the ideal, but of raising the ideal itself nearer to the New Testament standard. This might seem to be adding an additional burden to men; but Kierkegaard's aim was that under the increased pressure of this higher ideal, men might be more truly humbled to seek Divine grace. The Word of God only becomes alive and real for a man under the agony of an intense consciousness of sin and guilt. Where the standard of judgement is lowered and made relative, the consciousness of sin before God also becomes relative; and then Divine grace is spurned.

Kierkegaard sought to recall men to a sense of wonder and awe in the presence of the absolute God and His unspeakable grace and love. By his close study of the Bible and of Christian thought in all ages; by his thorough knowledge of human nature and of the ways of the human heart; above all, by deep meditation before God on the experiences of his own life, Kierkegaard sought to make known the ways of God to man. The motto he took for his own life was: 'All or Nothing.' The choice of God must be an absolute and unconditional one; or it is no choice at all. He set this same challenge before men. If God is not Lord of all, He is not Lord at all. In the face of his eternal destiny, man is confronted by the absolute Either/ Or. This is the great unconditional of life which stands firm and fast, the love of God for each single individual, a love which strives with man in his innermost existence, and will not let him go. God pleads with man to forsake time and to seek eternity, to venture out deeply into existence so that his real needs become apparent and can be met by God's grace.

Kierkegaard's interpretation of Christianity may seem at first to be a hard one, austere and harsh. But he knew full well the native shrewdness of the human heart in its way with God. Here was no mediating, compromising religion for the weak-hearted and for the pusillanimous. To such, Christianity is an offence and a scandal; it demands too much and gives too little. But in the New Testament Kierkegaard found a religion which was for real men, men of high intent and noble mind, for men ready for great adventure in the realm of the spirit, men who could face death with a song upon their lips, for their hearts were already filled with eternity. A desperate disease calls for a desperate remedy. The Sickness unto Death from which all mankind suffers is worse than the most deadly plague; for it kills a man and yet leaves him living. A palliative theology cannot answer to the desperate condition of man today. Nothing but a theology of the unconditional such as Kierkegaard sets forth, a theology which centres in the absolute of God, can avail for man's need today.

CHAPTER TWELVE

THE LIGHTHOUSE

The monastery is an essential dialectical factor in Christianity, and we need to have it there like a lighthouse, to gauge where we are—THE JOURNALS, 711

KIERKEGAARD lived and died a Protestant Lutheran Christian. But, as we have already noted, much interest has been shown by some Roman Catholic thinkers in his work. Was Kierkegaard by any chance a Roman Catholic at heart? Georg Brandes suggests that logically Kierkegaard confronts his readers with the Either/Or of Roman Catholicism or the total rejection of Christianity in any form. Some other writers have given it as their opinion that if Kierkegaard had lived longer, he would eventually have joined the Roman Catholic Church. Even Karl Barth asserts that on the problem of the *analogia entis*, which he takes as the dividing line between Catholicism and Protestantism, Kierkegaard is on the Roman side.

In spite of the weight of these opinions, we cannot get away from the fact that Kierkegaard was essentially a Protestant. It was with the deepest sincerity that in one of his last books he wrote: 'A man is justified only by faith. And therefore, in God's name, to hell with the Pope and all his auxiliary assistants.'[1] If we take the dividing line between Protestantism and Catholicism at the point where Martin Luther broke essentially with the latter, then it is on the conception of justifying faith that the difference is to be judged. On this basis there can be no doubt of Kierkegaard's position and true home.

But Kierkegaard was not satisfied with Protestantism as

[1] *SE*.202.

it was in his day. He saw much in Catholicism which appealed to him and which seemed to him to preserve, at least in theory, the Christian ideal of life in a much purer way than in Protestantism. Much as Kierkegaard admired Luther and his doctrines, he also saw and exposed the weakness of Lutheranism. Luther in his day and generation had to emphasize the doctrine of justification by faith alone as against the Roman doctrine of merit. But once Protestantism was established as the State religion, as it was in Denmark, the weakness of a one-sided emphasis on this doctrine became apparent.

Luther did not deny the necessity of good works. They are the fruit of a saving experience of Christ, but not the means of achieving merit before God for salvation. To Luther good works meant the transformation of personal character, since good works naturally flow from a changed heart. Kierkegaard, however, goes much farther. A mere transformation of character in 'hidden inwardness' is not enough. There must also be the transformation of a man's whole existence in the world, in imitation of the Pattern set by Christ in His early life. This is what Kierkegaard calls 'Reduplication'. The unconditional relationship of faith to God in Christ also means an unconditional dis-relationship to the world. God-affirmation means world-renunciation. Unless justification by faith alone is carried through in this way to its logical conclusion, Protestantism becomes 'a hiding-place for sheer paganism and epicureanism'.[2] Merely to say that one has faith in Christ in the heart is not enough. Even the best of good works can be counterfeited by the unbeliever.

On the one hand, Christian faith means the surrender of the self to God; utter self-denial and God-affirmation. On the other hand, it equally means denial of the world, a break with worldliness in every shape and form. To share in Christ's glory, we must first share in His sufferings,

[2] *J.*899.

which come through a refusal to be subject to the world. In the Christian life it is our task not to bring Christianity into harmony with our worldly existence, but to bring our existence into harmony with the life of Christ. The imitation of Christ is not just in His character, but in imitating His essential mode of existence on this earth. This is the absolute requirement of God for human existence. Christ renounced the world, the flesh, and the devil; He broke every tie that would hold him to the temporal; and in the light of the eternal He served God in humility, poverty, and self-abasement.

Kierkegaard points out that the Roman Church has preserved this ideal of the Christian life, and enforces it, outwardly at least, for its priests. Protestantism, however, has rejected it. When Luther broke with the Roman Church, he also abolished the monastery which in Catholicism was the visible sign and form of the Christian ideal for life. It was true that the monasteries were often corrupt. In that day they stood as the outward symbol of the doctrine of salvation by merit. Men entered them with the double motive of acquiring merit for the next world, and of enjoying the esteem and praise of men in this world. So Luther would have no monasteries, and he insisted that the Christian ideal was not that of the monk, but that of living a spiritual life amidst a wordly calling.

Luther's whole doctrine of justification by faith, however, depends upon the presupposition that the human conscience is thoroughly aroused by a deep sense of guilt, and awakened to its need of Divine grace. But, remove the pressure of the ideal requirement, namely, the imitation of Christ in His poverty, celibacy, and obedience, and how can the conscience be aroused sufficiently to seek grace in a real way? Where the soul is not deeply humbled under the absolute requirement of Christianity and where the sense of the unconditional is not felt, grace is taken in

INDEX OF PERSONS

INDEX OF SUBJECTS